# Goatfish / Cowtooth

Poems by Stephen Johnson

Kansas City   Spartan Press   Missouri

Spartan Press
Kansas City, Missouri
spartanpresskc.com

Copyright (c) Stephen Johnson, 2017
First Edition 1 3 5 7 9 10 8 6 4 2
ISBN: 978-1-946642-30-1
LCCN: 2017955532

Design, edits and layout: Jason Ryberg
Cover painting: John Hachmeister
Author photo: Sheila Montgomery
All rights reserved. No part of this publication may be reproduced or transmitted in any form or by any means, electronic or mechanical, including photocopying, recording or by info retrieval system, without prior written permission from the author.

Spartan Press would like to thank Prospero's Books, The Fellowship of N-finite Jest, The Prospero Institute of Disquieted P/o/e/t/i/c/s, Will Leathem, Tom Wayne, Jeanette Powers, j.d.tulloch, Jason Preu, Mark McClane, Tony Hayden and the whole Osage Arts Community.

"goat drinks a little gin in mid-afternoon and prevaricates" and "goat gets real good drunk and pontificates" first appeared in *Coal City Review*; "The Fortinbras Argument" first appeared in the *Kansas City Star;* "Invocation to John Brown" and "The Cleaning" first appeared in *Mikrokomos;* "Bullfrog Mythologies" first appeared in *Physics of Context*.

This book's section titles come from Robert Pogue Harrison's Forests: The Shadow of Civilization. In his introduction, Harrison writes, *In his New Science (1744) [Giambattista Vico] applied to ancient myths a genetic psychology that led him deep into the forests of prehistory in search of the origins of what he called the three 'universal institutions' of humanity—religion, matrimony, and burial of the dead* (3).

## CONTENTS

goatfish

cowtooth

**i. religion**

Bullfrog Mythologies / 1

Invocation to John Brown / 2

Reading the Bible Backwards He Returns
  to Paradise Under the Severe Gaze of
  Guardian Angels Brandishing Swords of
  Flame and the Awful Will of God / 3

During an Unscheduled Seven-Hour Delay
  In a Greyhound Bus Station, Spokane, WA / 6

A Faith / 7

Invective Concerning Wayward Anglers / 8

Home from the School for the Deaf,
  My Brother Speaks the Language of Animals / 10

All We Knew Was They Were Biting on
  Purple Worms and #6 Rooster Tails / 12

What News the Animal Delivers / 13

**In the Fish House** / 14

July Salmon Run, Nak Nek, Alaska / 15

What Was Said Behind the Smith
  Butcher Machine / 16

The Old-Timer Calculates a Day's Labor
  Against a Day's Wages and the Prophet of
  Time Entire Sets in Motion the Clock of the
  Lower Order of Angels / 17

Butcher's Etiquette / 19

Would You Believe Me if I Told You I Stood
   in a Fish House in Nak Nek, Alaska, Presiding
   Over Broken-Winged Salmon, Listening to
   Prayers Come from the Mouths of Fishes? / 21

**ii. Matrimony** / 23

Mapless / 24

Horses Swimming / 25

Consider the Earth, Us / 26

The Fortinbras Argument / 27

Unwinding / 28

My Love's a Cop / 29

On Her Husband's Return / 30

Adultury / 31

Rock, Paper, Water / 32

After Tonight I Will Have Written
   a Love Poem / 34

Talking in Your Sleep / 36

Talking in My Sleep / 37

**Ecce Capra: The Mad Sonnets** / 38

Ecce Capra / 39

goat drinks a little gin in mid-afternoon
   and prevaricates / 41

goat gets real good drunk
   and pontificates / 42

pandemonium poker / 43

goat figgers it's about time
   to sober up / 44

**bury your dead** / 45

If Youth is Wasted on the Young,
   Then Dying Beautifully is Wasted on the Old / 46

Trying to Recount Euclid's Axioms Before
   the Crucifix and the Vanishing Point that is
   the Father / 47

In the Nick of Time / 48

Hard / 50

One Hi-Ball, a Pack of Winstons and a
   Chevy Nova Idling Away in the Garage / 54

Clean Butchery / 55

Mind Under Matter / 58

Waking Up on the Stupid Side of History
   I Need a Coffee, I Need it Black, and I
   Need it Quick / 59

Bone Yard / 61

Spirit Level / 62

Leaning into a Calendar of the Pyramid
   at Chichen Itza, It's What the Heart Wants / 63

**iii. religion redux / 64**

goatfish / 65

cowtooth / 66

goatfish cowtooth / 67

*The forests have been cleared. Imagine yourselves in "religion, matrimony, and burial of your dead."*

--Robert Pogue Harrison

goatfish:

      grass and reed
           ember and pitch
                  pollen tongue lips spit

cowtooth:

      ochre and mud
          pumice and sponge
              water bowl knife lungs

i.

r
e
l
i
g
i
o
n

# Bullfrog Mythologies

Fling
your crazy legs wide
leap

the cow's
muzzle
as she

muddles
the rising
watermark

uncertain

hooves

sinking

Or
dive
inside

the moons
of her
eyes

impress
a mizzling
madness

## Invocation to John Brown

You're hanged well, John Brown, and the only one
    With that ox-eyed stare right out of King James.
        That rust In your beard is blood reefed on the wine-

Red plains of Kanzas.  Frothed and snagged, you fist
    Scripture from your lungs in fiery reverend cant.
        Who's to interpret your rent tongue?  You're the last

And first John who gospeled in Kanzas: the saint
    Excoriating brute flesh with an ox-hide strop,
        The penitent Jeremiah bent

On raising New Babylon.  Your vision: Rip
    America's slag-wasted body into pure
        Hosannahs; smelt the God-less dross; keep

His will hammered until the States curl over
    like Christ's nailed hands.  Work of the devil, child of
        God, this is my invocation to the grave: Sear

The Word into my skull.  Brand the brain *DEAD*,
    Relieved of guilt, Osawatomied, and penned
        Like pigs in your tin can-of-sass heart.  Bleed

Fear and decency, and I'll understand
    Your anthraxed rant.  No, we will go together down
        Into your Sodomized heart, together sound

the Marais de Cygne night, dark like us, one in sin.

## Reading the Bible Backwards He Returns to Paradise Under the Severe Gaze of Guardian Angels Brandishing Swords of Flame and the Awful Will of God

He says it like he found Jesus.
*You know they got this hazelnut creamer?*
*I shit you not this stuff is good.*
A week, seven days, he's been out after serving 10 of 15.
Talks at a rate that defies solitary confinement.
*I'm still up at 5 a.m.*
*I got this phantom bell in my head,*
*kicks me awake like an amputated leg.*
And every day he sits bolt upright,
straight as an inmate on surprise inspection.

A steel cot and mattress with stained ticking
first eased him into the Good Book.
One year later, the concentration of time
like a single nail tapped into his forehead.
Five years later, the expansion of time
like a bed of nails spaced too far apart.
*I Read it three times, and the last,*
*get this, backwards, so my eyes—blasted,*
*blinded, with the Revelations—*
*could be restored by the Gospels.*

A guy they called Preach laid Word
on his sorry pagan soul—
*Rebuilt my house, foundation of rock and all that,*
*but to get home I got to make that exodus,*
*wander the desert awhile, you know?,*
*living on manna, amening the madmen—*
and Shank writ it on him, tattooed
his back a tablet of eternal indemnity:
Gabriel and Michael, wings spread
fiercely upon each shoulder blade,
flaming swords crossed over the backbone,
the gates of the Garden just open.

*But the problem was the tiger.*
*Me and Shank we had different plans*
*before I got the old timey 'ligion,*
*so we had to figure a way*
*to work that tiger in, you know, symbolically.*
*He done this tiger from the backside,*
*like it's tearing into me and busting all my insides out.*
*Preach he loved that, went on about mysterious ways*
*and he says, Aw, symbols is easy, brother,*
*the beast he comes back, see?,*
*takes his rightful place beside the lamb.*
*That's all Biblical and whatnot.*

He's travelling on to Arizona to surprise his mother,
see his ex, divorced twice now
and hired full-time as a Macy's clerk.
His sight will grow lush again, green again.

He will take to calling her Eve, and she will not mind.
In fact, she might let him taste of the fruit once more.
Mornings, he will drink ten, count them, ten cups of
coffee, one for every year in, because he can.
He will pour hazelnut creamer like milk and honey.
He will spread his hands on the table, blind
as Lazarus in the dark, as Saul in the light.

## During an Unscheduled Seven-Hour Delay In a Greyhound Bus Station, Spokane, WA

A Malaysian Buddhist, and practicing tourist, suggests a totemic misappropriation.

## A Faith

Norman brings her out Thanksgiving—Our Lady
of Guadalupe.  He places her under
a sheltered frame of ¾ pine backed
with ply that keeps the space above her head.

Our Lady's white string of lights burns steadily
under the constant blink of a red *Noel*
he suspends faithfully each year by the low
eaves.  This year he wraps steel wire across her

outstretched benevolence, a barbed
necessity as the cracked wrist attests,
and one lost finger, never recovered,
shattered beyond the broken curb.

He had to.  How else could he save her
the wounds her upturned palms receive from kids?
He knows they are his son's friends who burn
away the night in a Nova, laughing

their eyeballs hot with Mad Dog 20/20,
rubbing together soft flesh of hands just warm,
knows Our Lady is prepared to suffer,
knows how these boys must tremble.

## Invective Concerning Wayward Anglers

It is truly living luxury.  Might as well be staying at
   the Radisson Meuhlbach.
The skillet's greased and the Coleman stove's waiting
   to be fired up in the morning for poor-man's eggs.
I got the tent up, boat in, and two lines wet already,
and here comes some silly son of a bitch with his son
   of a bitch son fishing my water.
The boy just finished off a Shasta Root Beer and bear
   claw, tossed the can rattling in the boat. His pop
   should have explained by the time sonny boy here
   was two that bass spook easy.  This water won't be
   good to fish again until next July, and here it is
   September.  So you tell me. What would you do?

Now I know you understand how I hope this breacher
   of good fishing etiquette has more sons and daughters,
   how I wish they all grow up to be fine, fine carp fisher-
   men and creek noodlers, and how I pray when they
   finally, finally cast their last bait upon the waters,
their bodies shall sink to the bottom of a DDT'd farm
   pond good for nothing but watering two-headed cows.
May copperheads wrap about their limbs.
May bottomfeeders pluck that silly-ass look out of
   their sockets. And may this man's children never know
   water, never know how it levels everything, above and
   below.

But this boy, this boy I do wish the very best.
May his liver never rot from a daily twelve-pack
  of Olympia.
May he be the prodigal son and develop a real talent
  for cutthroat trout and sockeye salmon.
May nothing but clean-water fishing fill his days.
May he travel far—Montana, Washington, Alaska,
  and farther still—far from Kansas, far from this
  fishing hole.
May he wade streams gracefully, cast skillfully with
  line strong and flies true.
May he luck into a record Chinook, and in that instant,
  oh, in the very moment of the perfect hook, may he
  splash blindly into a family of feeding Grizzlies.
May he come face to muzzle with the legitimate
  claim on that hole.
May he be crushed and ground into a tasty pâté.
And may his father never know of his son's fortune,
  good and ill.

The man with his boy gives me a wave.
Naturally, I touch the bill of my cap, say,
  *What are they biting on?*

## Home from the School for the Deaf,
## My Brother Speaks the Language of Animals

Friday night's feature presentation was *Planet of the Apes*
and Charlton Heston's enmeshed in a man-catcher's net.
If only he could free himself he'd kill a dozen gorilla
   warriors. It's pizza night. My brother and I devour our
   way into the bodies of beasts, rip into a Totino's
   Canadian bacon, extra cheese.
Oh, we'd seen plenty Mutual of Omaha's *Wild Kingdoms*.
Pumping our lungs was an African veldt wind,
and we gorged on the kill.
Our living room had been a snake pit, a croc-infested
   swamp, a gladiator's coliseum where we fought our
   battles with sword and spear and requisite barbarian
   grunts, cut each other's throats, hammed up Kirk
   Douglas's dimpled Spartacus and celebrated with *you
   were brave, my friend, and a noble opponent ...
   but ...* victories. He did ask how he was to hear
   the emperor, the call to glory, to no mercy.
So I taught him the standard thumbs-up-thumbs-down-
   on-an-imperial-whim-rule, signs that were less than
   he meant, but I like to think it prepared him for a
   lifetime's jabber and gesture and, years later, for a guy
   named Pete down at Handy Dan's, who said, *Oh, yeah,
   it's like playing charades.*
Did he say charades? My brother asked. Yes.
Tell him his mouth puckers up like a baboon's ass
   when he says *Oh*.

Yeah, Pete, just like charades.

But we are no longer boys, and we cannot pretend to those savage acts our mother had no business with, our sisters no traffic.

Ours is a discourse of commerce and civility.

But Colonel George Taylor's is the language of bewilderment.

When he speaks for the first time before his simian captors, *Get your stinking paws off me, you damn dirty apes!*, orangutans, gorillas, and chimpanzees rear back wide-eyed and gasping.

This filthy, this dumb, this brute animal, *he talks!*

## All We Knew Was They Were Biting on Purple Worms and #6 Rooster Tails

He didn't weigh sixty pounds, my brother,
yet somehow managed to finagle,
what our grandfather estimated
at fifty pounds itself, the rusted barrel
of a cement mixer up onto the tailgate.
For the first time I equated
a grown man scratching his head
with *Beats the shit out of me.*
Don't think we didn't investigate
for some means, a semblance
of pulley and rope, plywood ramp,

act of God even.  Nothing.
And since we were losing
daylight and good fishing,
we broke off our muttering,
left the hulk squatting
as concrete evidence
of our dumb astonishment
only to notice him gone again.
One of us would be sent,
fighting hackberry and Osage orange,
avoiding poison ivy and sumac,
to find him, deliberating a rear axle and driveshaft,
its removal from a wreck of brush and weeds.

## What News the Animal Delivers
*after Merwin*

A whitetail buck wilds the backyard
alert with hooves and twitching ears
stills the sun as fog grays the dawn

Waking as a man I know
spring is far off and the woods farther
Deer in passing mark it just so

as skunk and opossum
root around the tool shed
as the hawk shears the field mouse

move the animal in us
and still the human in us
sees the wild that remains

*In the Fish House*

## July Salmon Run, Nak Nek, Alaska

It's my job to wade waist deep
in dead fish. Chinook, sockeye,
and chum, an occasional sole
floundered into the drift nets,
trash fish in this business.
When the schools aren't running,
they give us odd jobs painting
rusted sheds that will rust again come winter.
Rather pay cheap wages to sober workers
than pull a man from low-tide mud flats
by his feet. Last night
about midnight, the sun equipoised
on the tundra, mosquitoes hatched
mad over stagnant seep, a young buck
out of south Texas took a tire jack
and boat blocks to the head. Over a girl,
an Inuit, out of the bush with her brothers
for summer canning and country bars.
Three days in the tender holds
of fishermen, the salmon have not lost
all their color, speckle gone mottled,
silver gray, a haze of carnation.
Blood runs in the brine.
Tubercular pink smears my waders.
At the end of an 18-hour day,
half buried, stunned, amazed,
I mutter something. About home.
A name gone strange.
A familiar meat with a foreign taste.

# What Was Said Behind the Smith Butcher Machine

Lazy assed mechanics, man, and the chiner it never
   goes down.
I pull two 8s and a deuce every godforsaken day
and they sit couch shift 24/7.
You know they got cable TV and cold beers
   in their room?
And I mean good American beer.
I seen a Budweiser can in the trash.
I need sleep.
When I knocked on their door,
on account of all the racket,
they threw a blanket over the TV, said, *What you want?*
Like I couldn't tell there was a TV under the blanket.
They left it on. I think they was drunk.
I got two hours sleep and a bad crick in my back.
And I'm tea-totaling fucking sober. I ain't going to make it.
Somebody round here has got to throw a wrench
   in the chiner.

# The Old-Timer Calculates a Day's Labor Against a Day's Wages and the Prophet of Time Entire Sets in Motion the Clock of the Lower Order of Angels

We know our rights and once our eight is done
we hit the time-and-a-half run. In the betweens
one break every two hours—by law, by god.
When you look upon the face of the clock
you may think you see the devil incarnate,
but you bear witness to I am that I am.
Six or one-half-dozen the other is a blasphemous lie
perpetrated by messengers false and minions infernal.
24 hours is not a day, and 15 minutes never a
   quarter-hour.
That you can count as gospel. Consider:
at nine minutes til, you take a piss break.
That's six minutes gravy. When you get
back to the line it's like that three don't even exist.
Erase it from the ledgerbook;
you know what time it is.
Everbody knows what time it is.
You got your fifteen, that's settled,
but you don't go nowhere near the floor
until 16, 16 ½ after—I do admit the math gets a little
   fuzzy depending how itchy the line leader is,
   whether or not he whacked it last night.

He might be doing the clap-happy marine bit:
*Suit up, boys and girls, we ain't here to eat donuts,*
*we're here to clean fish guts.*
Sometimes you call time and take the loss.
After desmocking and washing up to the elbows
you got 12 max remaining. That's no time for a fireside
   chat, just some goof-balling, a joke on the line-leader,
that hitch he's got in his get-along on account
of too much fish-head soup.
On the regular? To think we're going to suit up,
be back on floor at 15 after, not a second more,
is horeseshit plain and simple.
You take the pre-nine, 15, and post-three,
that's 27 out of 15. I'd like to see
a normal human being shave the skin that thin.

Around here we may not work miracles,
but we do work wonders.
We make time out of no-time,
we kill time with all our time,
and we execute these wonders
with the authority, the severity,
the ferocity of god's best killing crews.

# Butcher's Etiquette
### --Nak Nek, Alaska, 1999

Done with this century, its end
drawn quick and tied to the next,
a blood knot cinched tight and clipped trim
to ease the pass through that narrow eye.
The salmon we take make their last run
to continue on.  When a rare one
survives the nets and haul,
three days in the belly of a tender,
and the unceremonious chute and drop
into brine-filled tanks,
it is cradled alive to the river
courtesy of the master butcher.
The rest of us, gangplank workers and factory drudges,
leave our stations to see the resurrection and return,
grace delivered in rubber boots and a plastic apron.
The chining machine is silenced, the slime line
abandoned, and the holding tanks, where I am charged
with watching over a congregation of stunned eyes
staring back at unfinished business,
are left to their quiet keep.
We turn out a ragged procession, many of us
cranked on amphetamines, addle-brained pilgrims
half way through a 16-hour shift,
most of us high, few sober, all weary and ready for
what?  We do not know.  A break along the way,
a respite before the century to come?

The master butcher squats
at the edge of the fish house dock
like a Stone Age mother holding her child
for its first immersion.
So that is it.  We gather to witness
this miracle, this slick and living
bloom delivered unto the waters.
But one of us, eyes dilated and new to all this business,
points farther out, some crumple or shred on the surface.
A beluga hunting upriver, one of the Inuits tells us.
We gawk at it rise and disappear and rise again
like white thread in a raveled hem stitching or unstitching.

# Would You Believe Me if I Told You I Stood in a Fish House in Nak Nek, Alaska, Presiding Over Broken-Winged Salmon, Listening to Prayers Come from the Mouths of Fishes?

Dead they persist with a pedant's devotion to dogma,
an uncanny instinct to hurry up and wait,
to turn madly down in a voluptuous,
feathery, proselytizing school of one.
They are vacuumed from the tenders of fisherman
  moored on the river.
They are sucked from bloated bellies up conduits and
  over our heads through a machined network of
  rivers, a city block of industry designed to
  dismember the animal.
I climb the ladder and stride above it all in rubber
  waders and suspenders until it is time to descend.

I glide like some lower order angel on corrugated air
  and steel twisted above the great briney tanks where
  they rain down chinook, sockeye, sole broken-
  winged and lame, their bulleted bodies the color of
  daguerreotype carnations.
Nine days straight on eighteen hours a day, time bevels
  horizons, casts a wan slant on our midnight's labor,
  tilts the polar disc at our killing.
The ice-house spreads its wings and broods over
  the river.

And from the brine and blood the fishes issue one
   oceanic whisper, one skinned and gilled suspuration,
   one puckered and fluked, one beaked and feathered,
   clawed and tailed, one tentacled, pincered, one sieved,
   scaled, finned, hammered, one pressed, fingered,
   fleshed, toed, boned, one throated, one mouthed,
   one lipped, one prayer:
Keep us. Give us our prey and feed us daily. Keep us
   from sunlight and air. Keep us from the barbed hooks,
   the meshed nets, the vulgar buoys.
Keep us from the ropes and pulleys, the callused hands,
   the horn-rimmed hands.
Keep us in tide and stream.
Keep us in darkness and depth.
Keep us from sailor's ears and the loving kisses
   of their captains.
Keep us Keep us Keep us Keep us Keep us.

*ii.*

*matrimony*

## Mapless

I would make of your body
a new world unchartered,
unbound by nation, state,
the wild commons,
a grotto of linden and laurel
left to your own devices,
but for my desire.

## Horses Swimming

No wonder children grow up inveterate liars.
We tell them the dark is nothing
more than the absence of light.
We tell ourselves dreams are nothing
more than fantastic creatures issued forth
from the meres and glens of our waking lives,
and that we can send them scampering
with torches of reason.
There is so much I need to be true:
that these cut and quartered oranges on a blue plate
are sun enough to light this room and us;
that travelling is pilgrimage,
and settling building a life together;
that choices we make are choices we make.
I need to believe you when you say
you miss the hardwood forests,
hate the desert; that iron in the rock
rises to the surface to better define gravity;
that it is not the sun's trick
of attracting all things to toppling.
I need to believe the story of horses
swimming from Chincateague to Asateague,
that every year they leave only for a season.
I need to believe who told me that story and why.

## Consider the Earth, Us

At this speed you would think we understand
we're going nowhere fast.
The world burns in its ecliptic,
loses its roundness in the heat of its run.
The miles we traveled, baby.
With the stress our structural integrity
endures, you'd think
we would have broken up long ago.
We need to get out of this desert.
These prophets and their trials by sun and rock.
When they complain,
and they always complain,
they do so zealously, grievously,
with the authority of hard elements,
the credibility of camel hair and locusts.
No wonder they're cantankerous.
A wonder they believe
in anything at all.  Their word
is iron in the stone,
fire on the Mount,
water gone from the valley.
We've been living with this handful of dust
too long.  Let us go now
to the land of lichen and fern.
We will lay down our bed, and we will build our house.
We will live out our time among pine and shade.
Let us commit our bodies to the cool, green flame.
Let us speak no hasty word.
Let us delight in our earthy immolation.

## The Fortinbras Argument

> *--I do not know*
> *Why yet I live to say 'This thing's to do'...*
>
> Hamlet 4.4.

We rise Sunday morning above the grave
history of this house, when we can reason
the routine task of tending our garden
as an act of knowing we know we live.
With nothing to determine our ruin
but a few weeds, we find it easy with no
Quantrill, no Absalom, no grand woe
to endure, no Claudius to act upon.
All we need not to fall is make the most
of what's left, of what's not yet buried,
and no more.  We'll make no more of the dead
than eggshells, thoughtlessly tossed to compost.
Then why do we, like that doubtful Dane, pause
before the act, smell the stink of what is, was?

# Unwinding

Funny, this drive taken to undo
routine, the argument the night before, the morning's
tangle. But it was the unexpected going beyond
the Flint Hills, into Post Rock country, where
fence posts cut from native limestone
remain rooted like tongues,
that undid everything.
*Let's just unwind,* as if that were the most original
thing to say, as if our bodies were coiled
forgotten and unused under a pile of corrugated tin,
waiting as barbwire to be stretched miles horizon tight.
I had to taste one, a stone post, like a salt-lick.
She laughed at this gesture,
childish and done on a whim.
We said nothing when this one ended
beside I-70 with a photo of us and a sign
that read AMERICAN BISON PRESERVE
but no bison in sight. We posed, angled
toward the vast plains, her hands in the air,
me scratching my head, both our bodies
saying, *See? We've been had again.*

## My Love's a Cop

with a flashlight
tapping the driver's window
asking for i.d.
*I thought you were a couple of kids,*
*drinking maybe,* my love says.
*Well, I'd rather not bother.*
*There's a place or two up the road*
*where you can do what you want,*
*you just can't do it here.*

## On Her Husband's Return

She smiles
brief as a blade
rests on the skin
of a trout
before easing
into giving.

# Adultury

The shape of my hand lifts from your belly,
a stream-wet paw-print from a sun-heated stone.

## Rock, Paper, Water

1

Azuko folds 10,000 years, holds
them in her palm: *origami no tsuru:*
paper crane. It is a gift
of longevity. It is a myth as thin
as this island, gentle
as its continent-shouldered curve.

Sound as *banzai:* 10,000 years.

I wait for the words to come.
I want them to wash over the tongue
with the ease of *mizu:* water
over stone. But I'm only good with the O
and its hollow echo. The tongue trips
over the rest untried into its dry bed.

Spring all around us,
the rice fields have been flooded
and still we listen to the trickle
of water down hillside and canal.
So much water: mildew grows
in my closet silent as paper wings,
patient as stone,
enduring somewhere between.

2

*Place a cold river-stone on your tongue
and you will swear it's melting,* she tells me.

Plucked from the vocabulary of mountains,
content in its vowel-rounded hardness,

the stone impresses a sense of giving
without loss, of speaking without voice.

She holds it as if to measure
the sound of melting

then places it on my tongue,
this shared element of the foreign

for the foreigner in a land
wild as banzai and quiet as bonsai.

*Ishi no gawa,* she says.
Her oblations complete,

we skip our small os over the river,
quick as taps of the tongue

alive with the taste of sound.

# After Tonight I Will Have Written a Love Poem

and would like to include you.
I will have cleared a space for your name on line 39,
but then that might be too obvious, and a poem should
   unfold like an origami fortune teller.
So I will let you choose where it goes, and I won't look.
As for your name, you may use the one given,
Michael, Brian or Adam will do,
or Chloe, Ashley, Elizabeth. They are all fine,
but so too is a parlor game name, a Professor Plum
   or Miss Scarlet.
Whether you think of yourself as a Maryanne or a
   Madame X,
as a Lester McNester or a Brock Remington,
it is safe here. It's a love poem.
In a year or ten or more, maybe you will remember
whose hand you were holding, whose you weren't,
what lover you were going home with,
the one to whom you will have said,
after lovemaking, *See? Now that's poetry, baby!*
Then you will have waxed on or waxed off about
the moon, how it shines through the venetian blinds,
because careful research tells us one in five poems
with love or sex or a bedraggled breakup (too much?)
has a moon or at the least a surrogate O;
and you will have said *the blinds are sifting the moonlight
over our bodies,* which is not quite right, because what

the blinds really do if angled just right
is cut the light like slices of cheese;
and you will have wished there had been curtains,
say of muslin, which is a weave too plain for erotic poetry
but a word sensuous as a Provencal song,
    exotic as a Turkish harem.
You will have lit up or not, ordered Chinese or not,
stayed in bed or pressed your palm to your head,
remembering something, anything, pressing enough
    to excuse your exit.
In any case, all you have to do is lift one word
    in this poem.
It can give you anything.  It can be multi-foliate,
a *fleur-de-lis* of Latinate pretensions: loquacious,
    lascivious, alliteration.
It can be Greek: eros, philosophy, or poem.  It can be
    German: ox, or church or fuck.
Perhaps Arabic, or Persian or Sanskrit: orange, minaret,
    muezzin.
I invite you to lift your secret word, maybe dig a little into
    the line below,
and place your name there like a token, a relic, a map,
and tap it down: word, name and poem.
And take care.  Tonight, when the one you love,
or don't, leans over in the sliced cheese light
to decipher the silent cant your lips give shape to,
already you may have been forgetting
whether you whisper the name given or the name made.

## Talking in Your Sleep

Tell me you are far, far away, not in place but in time,
   not in body but in mind.
Tell me you travel in tongues of your own kind,
not alien but strange and away.

Tell me when you are nearly away, gone and
   no longer my kind,
when I no more remain in your waking mind,
call to me in that strange way.

Tell me how, tell me what to stay.

## Talking in My Sleep

Last night cicada droned the end of summer
in a mad Morse Code;

crickets gathered around the Judas tree
that will not blossom or bleed until Spring;

NPR reported a Japanese koi worth $3000
went missing from a Wichita garden pond.

I'm lost in Kansas which I've told you is more than
place, *it's a philosophy, a state of mind, a religion.*

I need to get back to here.
Orion up at 4 a.m.,

and you still in my bed.
I need to get back to that too.

A dream when I fell back to sleep, before sunrise,
arm wrapped about you:

koi, hundreds, thousands, shimmering in a cricket and
cicada racket of summer; a hunter preying for winter.

This morning I have mistaken all of Kansas.
I am unwise, unsettled, and heretical.

# Ecce Capra: The Mad Sonnets

*And he shall set the sheep on his right hand,
but the goats on the left.*
                    *--Matthew 25:33*

# Ecce Capra

You can't exactly call stolen
this rock I took from a local
college campus.  It is native
limestone, and I, too, have quarried

> *goat*
>
> > *entered life last night, horned*
> > *ruminant clattering*
> > *across the roof's clay tiles.*
> > *i am haunted by goats.*

Kansas for a deep-bedded life-
time, which is a relative matter.
So, I submit: this rock is blood.
Exoneration in toto,

> > *i am told it is a blessing*
> > > *to enter the dreams*
> > *of animals*
> > > *furious with living.*

a priori allegations,
is all that I demand.  The real
caper was stacking it here,
a cairn among pulpits.  The stone's

*so, fashioned goat's head*
  *from rope, shard of clay*
*locust seed pod, and one*
  *stone the shape of animal.*

free to go:  habeas corpus.

*the work's come*
  *and gone, totem,*
*dawn, poem.*

# goat drinks a little gin in mid-afternoon and prevaricates

> *And if his offering be a goat, then he shall*
> *offer it before the Lord.*
>                             --Leviticus 3:12

i'm a beast    a goat
a piece of meat
with a shaggy coat
an animal    a brute

unwilling    to reason
to try that treason
which tempts a man
to know    to want

all    the same as sane
can be    a kid's need
of milk    and blood
drunk    like me
                split-

hoofed
        i eat rubber and tin
i pay for all but one
                sin

## goat gets real good drunk and pontificates

> *And [Isaac] said, Behold the fire and the wood:*
> *but where is the lamb for a burnt offering?*
> --Genesis 22:7

besides it was a ram that fell for that scam
when god or some angel or other stayed
old abram's hand    so this is god's chosen
i'd have given my beard to get inside
the old man's head    jesus he had some nerve
had the kid trundle up his own bundle
of sticks even    told him to put the knife
to stone    grind it good he said    an angel
will guide your hand like the edge of heaven
where all good boys go    grind it sharp as bone
and sweet as innocence on the tongue

but i'm too dumb to taste that guilty sting
and drunk though not so dumb as glad    glad as hell
i got my beard    glad as hell i'm not that ram

## pandemonium poker

don't let anyone tell you otherwise
it weren't no calf they fashioned from precious
gold absconded from a hot and heathen land
of obelisks odalisques copper skinned
pharaohs    it was the kid himself graven
beard hoof and horn by a lost people driven
to pick some god like manna    listen
mono and polytheism crystals
vortexes love daylight savings social
drinking self-improvement the Big Bang
no Bang Chaos Theory and everything
they don't understand which is just about
everything but to believe in believing
deal those bone cards    cuz i'm placing a bet

goat figgers it's about time
to sober up

> *And [Isaac] said, Thy brother came with subtlety,*
> *and hath taken away thy blessing.*
> --Genesis 27:35

Not so stupid really to cast away his birthright,
chicken bones not fit for beasts, let alone human
consumption, but for a thief, yes, and next of kin

dragged from the bowels by the heel, cursed to clean
living and milky skin.  A plain man of the tent, happy
with bare acres and vulgar enterprise, that foul

labor bent on breaking bodies of the world.  And whose
bodies are these anyway?  Our hero's, with red hair
and hunter's stride?  Our master thief, pottage pourer,

the one who earned the fingertip power of God,
thrown for a limp with shrunken thigh, touched muscle,
angel wound?  Though our hero did ask, when ready

to crush his brother's clavicle, winged scapula,
splayed lungs, wouldn't we all like to be touched, a little?

*iii.*

bury

your

dead

## If Youth is Wasted on the Young,
## Then Dying Beautifully is Wasted on the Old

We begin burying ourselves as children
when pretend-dying from gunshot,
toppling then tumbling dramatically down
a green hill choked with dandelions.
If our T-shirts and skin yellowed with the crush of petals
or if we POOFed airborne with our flailing bodies
specter-winged seeds, I cannot remember.

# Trying to Recount Euclid's Axioms Before the Crucifix and the Vanishing Point that is the Father
*after Bishop*

Not losing so much, that's the disaster.
It's years since ninth grade geometry
so I don't believe I could prove a square

a square if Euclid himself were here.
I did not lose a little faith in study.
Not losing so much, that's the disaster.

Think you can teach a boy how to measure
the father, son, and ghostly mystery
out of curved infinity into a square?

I came close once in the triangular
logic of Christ to a mastery—
not losing so much, that's the disaster—

over the nothing that became the father,
the mathematical uncertainty.
A life should not fit easily a square,

a rectangle. If Euclid were here
he'd set me straight. Might say, *It's clear
not losing so much, that is, the disaster
is never knowing what lines make (break) the square.*

# In the Nick of Time

I have no business
with you
and your tattoo,

the ourobouros
coiled about your navel.
I am not crawling

on hands and knees.
This is not the inner sanctum
of the Lascaux cave.

This indigo totem
is not plunging
into the center

of the body
of the universe.
Your belly is not

the fire-
scarred tableau,
not smoke and pigment

traced with breath.
If I could unflesh
ink and needle,

uncoil scale and fang,
I would cast it
in light and shadow.

It could kill a man
in his unmarked skin.

## Hard

> *To drive a car into and out of the garage all you got to do is pull straight in and pull straight out. Not Elsie. She maneuvers.*
>
>> —Verde Smith, commenting on the universally accepted principles of garage parking as compared with the particular parking habits of Elsie Smith one week after the incident, when tempers had cooled some

With a geometric convergence of point and angle beyond axiomatic reckoning, Elsie Mae backed her Nova 350 Hatchback out of the garage and positioned the elbow bend of the left rear bumper into the passenger door of Smitty's Chevy Impala station wagon. It was remarkable. As a ten-year-old who did not know the difference between gas pedal and brake pedal, I was witness, and that was enough. But this was Saturday, and August, and the ballgame was on the radio, and Elsie's brothers and sisters were there for beers and hi-balls and Braun-schweiger sandwiches. They too were witnesses, and that was more than enough.

On these Saturdays the garage doors were opened wide, the cars pulled out, and box fans set around lawn chairs. Habitually frugal, this depression-era generation preferred the shade and breeze of the garage, even with the smells of leaked 30-weight oil and the dessicated remains of chicken livers hard

-tacked to #8 fishing hooks, to running the air conditioner upstairs or worrying over condensation rings on the coffee table.

They were veterans, and smokers-in-earnest since the age of thirteen. I was still pulling tube socks up to my knees. We were all of us collectively awed by the impossibility, the excitement and the mystery of it all. Great aunts and uncles with names like Genevieve and Ruth, Clarence and Bud, the kind of names you expect to hear in diners over $1.99 a plate specials and see on pocket patches at filling stations that never even heard of self-serve, people with these names made a concerted effort to get at the where-fors and the why-hows. They looked and they looked, lifted prescription eye glasses to foreheads and squinted and, when that didn't help, dropped them back to where they had been in the first place, and squinted.

They peered into that space and time of crushed metal, these Euclidean pagans, as if to debunk the catholic trifecta or discover the Aleph. And not with a little joy. You could not plot and graph a less conceivable trajectory, could not predict according to any known calculus this heretofore never accomplished phenomenon, not in the natural world, not in this narrow, rectilinear matrix of a two-car drive. The nearly true and almost perfect right angle is best described as immaculate. My word now, not theirs then.

There was much bending over and straightening up and someone saying, *Huh.* Verde, politic as always, *Could've happened to anyone. I parked too close to Elsie's side anyway, maybe.* And Clarence, not so politic, *Naw, Smitty, you're practically in the neighbor's yard, killing their grass. She had plenty of room.* And still they looked, and she, the outlier, did not, and called them all sonsabitches from the breezy shade of the garage. Aunt Genevieve backed down the entire drive all the way to the street and then some, so as to get perspective, and filed her report: *It's something alright.*

Elsie Mae Cole, Elsie Mae Johnson, Elsie Mae Smith. Born 1917, died 1982. Cause of life: dustbowl parents poor as . . . well; pretty boy George Brett batting .465 for three miracle months; and Erica Kane perduringly glamorous in the forever of Pine Valley. Cause of death: brothers and husbands; grandbabies; arthritic knees, compliments of Western Auto shipping and receiving; and tar black and cobalt blue lungs.

Elsie Mae, if I had my druthers I would druther you up heavens of garages, I would line up all your days in eternity like Braun-schweiger sandwiches, like Old Crow and Ginger Ale hi-balls, like cartons of Winston 100s, the soft packs because you tuck them in your bra when you wear one, like cans of Schlitz Malt Liquor, I need not say by the case, like house dresses, what you called dusters, hung up in your closet, the ones you wore all day every day even to Safeway.

I'd line up your curlers and your dentures and your daytime stories, every affair tawdry, noble, or desperate, every amnesia episode, every surgery room trauma, every murder, every long lost twin come back from—what else?—the dead. You'd have it. All.

In the name of the chrome-plated bumper, the rack-and-pinion steering, and the holy disc brake, I give you a Stonehenge of 1972 Chevy Impala station wagons, four door, cornflower blue, and bought used, and for all of eternity you could back into each and every god-blessed one of them, hard.

## One Hi-Ball, a Pack of Winstons and a Chevy Nova Idling Away in the Garage

He slipped from us
as easily as a white-bellied carp
jumps from the water, never to drop back.

## Clean Butchery

My father is a fish:  he
swims alone; in open

wounds.  This is how I
this is how i remember

him.  goggle-eyed through
garage windows; regreasing oar locks,

patching a troublesome hole
in a john-boat that hasn't seen water

in two summers; deadpan practical;
useless.  this is how

\*

i want to remember him:  surrounded
by swamp oak and scrub, a tangle

of poison sumac and a copperhead
gone to shade; he's chosen

this clearing for its table of shale
shouldered from the dirt, its

perfect brevity.  A low bough dances
with the weight of a fine catch.  He

unhooks one, strips it
of the clean white meat.  (but this

is what i cannot) remember:  how
his memory thickens

into the oils of Hieronymous Bosch.
how the airy plunge and pull

of aquatic muscle has turned abattoir
into gallows.  how fins

grow legs and arms; how fish-headed
they serve a dire need

\*

I have come to think of myself
as a master of clean butchery,

competent wielder of thin knives.
A fine life this, devoted

to what he taught,
to what feels like instinct

though it is not, no more
than a well-practiced waltz

or an ear trained to the spiccato
of fry skimming the surface,

those small lives that move in a body,
splinter into one last act.

And finer still the ear
tuned to the catch,

dancing to some heaven,
music, dream of water.

## Mind Under Matter

It would not die.
After two hours
we pulled it
from the ice-chest,
its tail still
swishing the ice
like a brother-in-law
groping for a Coors Light.
It took an ice-pick
eventually through the head,
a cavern I imagined
nascent with moss-
green illumination,
a marine grotto
expunged of human light.
A spelunker's nightmare:
expecting darkness,
dropped into that bend
of animal matter
and plumb out of rope,
the sky-blue eye-hole
shrinking to a distant
will-o-the-wisp,
he finds himself
doing something
he has never done before,
pounding his chest for air,
kicking at the ground not there.

# Waking Up on the Stupid Side of History I Need a Coffee, I Need it Black, and I Need it Quick

*November 9, 2016*

Pit of the eye, dim.
Skull sulk.
Spine socket grind.
Spilled pills
like a hag's bones
rattled out a bone cup.
Chemical, dark,
sub-coccyx drop.
My weather foul,
my temper inclement,
my demographics gone
downright simple.
I'm trying to be politic
but somebody's got to pay.
And I don't mean
in a skinny cap
triple shot decaf
hazelnut dash
with a dollop
of whip cream
and chocolate sprinkles
hold up the godforsaken line
kind of way.

No.
I mean
I'm studying this,
with purpose, with principle.
turning inward and downward,
getting subterranean and troglodytic,
maybe even a little lower, a little darker.
These are pressing times.
I might have to get downwrong presidential.

# Bone Yard

*(found poem in a letter from Elizabeth, a friend)*

I took the dogs to the bone yard
last night.  All the snow made it lovely.
We were in the back plots
when someone locked the gates.
I had to toss one dog over the fence
and coax the other bigger and smarter one
into making the jump.

## Spirit Level

The old men toss perch and blue gill on the bank
where they cant and tack on their live
slick before drying in the sun.
Sometimes the old men reckon short,
figure more than a few slide down the pitch,
skew mud in a finger's breadth of water.
A chance tail flick and gill flex flips one or other
deep enough to right itself and make
back for the spawning bed.  In clear water,
the bottom looks like a corn field hoax,
circles and circles scutted clear of moss.
The moon hung gravid last night and tonight the
old men will keep at it long as the sunfish over-spawn.
It's a season they watch measured and regular
until sunrise turns shoreline and sky spirit level.

# Leaning into a Calendar of the Pyramid at Chichen Itza, It's What the Heart Wants

The washing machine decides it is the heart.
So the dryer wants to be the cardiac arrest
and the garbage disposal the final lurch.
Bread knives the ritual scalpel,
teaspoons the splayed fingers,
utility drawer the cracked sternum pried open.

The spin cycle hums like a hummingbird
flitting about the lavender flowers of a jacaranda.
Now the plastic marigolds have big ideas.
The curly-cue crazy straws
want to straighten out and get serious,
to be the beak that draws the nectar.

The souvenir chopsticks from Kyoto,
four pair of jade and plum
each wrapped a finger's width
of cherry blossom pastel and faux-gold filigree,
are surprisingly humble.
They wish to be the hollow bones.

religion

redux

goatfish:

   see how the cottonwood leans
      into the lightening of its love
         not to craze the patterned sky

   but the bowl unbroken
      we read our futures in

cowtooth:

    see too how the child
        reaches for the mother's mouth
            not to catch the breath

    but the whale song
        we ride the current of

goatfish cowtooth:

    let us cut two limbs of ash
    walk out there

Stephen Johnson is a Senior Lecturer in the English Department at the University of Kansas. He has published in *Puerto del Sol, Coal City Review, Physics of Context, Mikrokosmos*, and the *Kansas City Star*. He earned how to cuss from his grandmother, to read from the old timey testaments, and to write from carpenters, mechanics, and fishermen.